Into the New World

Also by Robert Schultz

War Memoranda: Photography, Walt Whitman, and Memorials, with Binh Danh

Ancestral Altars, with art by Binh Danh

We Were Pirates: A Torpedoman's Pacific War, with James Shell

The Madhouse Nudes

Winter in Eden

Vein Along the Fault

Wonderland: New & Selected Poems by Sarwat Zahra,
translated from the Urdu with Rizwan Ali

INTO THE NEW WORLD

Poems

Robert Schultz

INTO THE NEW WORLD
Poems

Copyright © 2020 Robert Schultz. All rights reserved. Except for brief quotations in critical publications or reviews, no part of this book may be reproduced in any manner without prior written permission from the publisher. Write: Permissions, Slant Books P.O. Box 60295, Seattle, WA 98160.

Slant Books
P.O. Box 60295
Seattle, WA 98160

www.slantbooks.com

HARDCOVER ISBN: 978-1-63982-082-5
PAPERBACK ISBN: 978-1-63982-081-8
EBOOK ISBN: 978-1-63982-083-2

Cataloguing-in-Publication data:

Names: Schultz, Robert.

Title: Into the new world: poems / Robert Schultz.

Description: Seattle, WA: Slant Books, 2020.

Identifiers: ISBN 978-1-63982-082-5 (hardcover) | ISBN 978-1-63982-081-8 (paperback) | ISBN 978-1-63982-083-2 (ebook)

Subjects: LCSH: Poetry. | American poetry. | American poetry — 21st century. | Vietnam War, 1961–1975 — Poetry. | United States — History — Civil War, 1861–1865 — Poetry. | War poetry, American.

Classification: LCC PS3569.C5535 I5 2020 (print) | LCC PS3569.C5535 (ebook)

Manufactured in the U.S.A.   OCTOBER 18, 2021

For Rigel and Axel, the future

No weekends for the gods now. Wars
flicker, earth licks its open sores....

Pity the planet, all joy gone
from this sweet volcanic cone;
peace to our children when they fall
in small war on the heels of small
war—until the end of time
to police the earth....

>   —Robert Lowell,
>   *from* "Waking Early Sunday Morning"

CONTENTS

I
When the Magnitude of the Possible Dawned | 3
Waking | 11
Marriage Fires | 12
Two or Three Dreams of Spring | 14
Black Velvet | 17
Sight and Distance | 19
Libretto for the Fall of the Year | 20
Winter in Eden | 22
Into the New World | 23
Disaster Movies | 25
Jan Brueghel the Elder's *A Woodland Road with Travelers* | 26
Not with a Bang, but a Tweet | 27
On Forsythia Overhanging a Slate Wall | 28

II
Gettysburg | 31
Amulet | 32
Necklace with Daguerreotype | 33
In Vietnam | 35
Drifting Souls | 36
Camouflage | 37
Green Man | 39
Vietnam Veterans Memorial, Night | 40
Khmer Rouge | 42
The Photographed | 43
Duty | 45
Up from Its Ground the Water | 47
The Botany of Tuol Sleng | 48
The Chankiri Tree | 49
Flowers of the Field | 50

III
The Varieties of Religious Experience | 53
The Highest Emblem in This Cipher of the World | 55
Thoreau, in Spring, at the Railway Embankment | 57
Chanticleer | 59
The Butterfly Portrait | 60

IV
The Morning News | 65
Elegy | 66
The Day after Charlottesville We Decide
    to Dig Out the Quince | 67
In a Field of Weeds | 69
Analysis | 70

Note | 73
Acknowledgments | 75

I

WHEN THE MAGNITUDE OF THE POSSIBLE DAWNED

I.

Last night we were lost. This morning
The back yard argues, as ever,
All pain is minor and passing.
Solid light, in its blocks and slabs,
Displaces vague fears, the night
Benign, domestic beneath trim shrubs.
By this light I'm stripping wild vines
From the plum, while its blossoms
Snow and the vines haul back, perverse
And muscular, tearing at last.
The grass throbs brighter the deeper
I breathe, and the season burns.
How surely the year finds its way
Toward spring, where Sally kneels
In the lettuce rows, a streak of clay
Like rouge on one cheek. Beside her
Schuyler careens and falls, inspects
A red clod, and rises again, his face
Aglow from within. So the day
Wheels by. And I am the watchful
Husbandman at evening here on a spinning
Ball when the green lawns tilt and night
Spills out from hedges and trees.

2.

In dissolving night, when all is possible,
Sky a cauldron of stars distending
To spew the planets or melt them down,
The lights of creation and decreation
Sparkle inseparably. Here by my son,
While rapid creepers retake the plum
And Sally pitches in troubled sleep,
I keep my watch

Through dangerous hours
When the night light's glow
Throws a nimbus about
My viral, incendiary boy.

His hot skin burns me.
Asleep, he leans in a sprinter's pose
While I kneel on the floor,
Sponging him down from 104.

This bomb is smart,
Homing its fire to the heart.

Bare on the Earth in this little room
Where the moment crests and I waken
Anew, again and again,
What may not happen?

Pray without ceasing.

*

Bless Aaron Bobb,
Who, my son's age,
Has died of a cancer
Strangling his heart.

Relieve his parents
Of their wildest rage
Which seeks an answer
Beyond all art.

3.

When the magnitude of the possible
Dawned—a morning doubly brilliant—
Many were so near they vanished instantly.
Others ran to the city's rivers, naked
But indistinguishable, woman from man.
As a black rain fell on the fires, the wounded
Dug for the buried wounded.

"Although we were lying side by side on the stairs,
We did not recognize each other.
He seemed unable to open his eyes or mouth
For the swelling of his burns, but he said somehow:
'Are you Mr. Matsumuro?' It was Yoshimoto,
And he knew me, too, when I spoke."

After the sickness and mourning, the spiking
Temperatures, bodily ruin unspeakable,
Grief and listlessness cupping the loss,
Survivors slipped out of gloves
Of themselves, sloughed off old surfaces,
Suffered grafts and reconstructions, and lived
With explosives buried inside.

4.

Especially after the acreage fires
The burr-oak thrives, its jack-box

Seeds tripped loose by the heat.
We tell ourselves such facts

As we can, to redeem charred waste,
And we note tough weeds scrabbling

Quick on a bank dozed clear.
The first mean vines knit up

A deep gouge, making soil for the next
Growth in line. New seeds more delicate

Follow, succession leading through pines
To beech, to this hardwood stand where

The shady floor is a powder of leaves,
Inviting and cool.

How spacious the bottomless sky
Appears from where I lie

In leafmeal and spines.
Trunks aim high toward the vanishing

Point where a star will appear
And tug all night on the buried dead.

By morning fingers, slender
And white, will have broken the loam.

Runners will leaf and at bushes
Or windfalls their tendrils loop

To entangle and climb,
To consume with a fire of their own.

Though soil is ash,
And I stretch myself over strata of bones,

Does the pea-vine climb less securely up?
Is the honeysuckle annulled?

I will rest myself in this undergrowth,
Serene as the ferns, the columbine, moss,

Clematis and grass—as the whole
Unconscious world in which

The moment is full
And unhistorical.

5.

Out from this chapel, its green
Enfolding sacristy quieting
All it surrounds—the weavings
Of grass, composures of weeds,
The scent of mint from certain
Crushed leaves, above it all
Hypnotic wavings of trees acircle—
Out from this chapel yet something
Reaches from me toward my life
In the intricate flames of destruction
And love.

6.

Out from the oak in the fireplace grate
Heat and light uncoil in tongues,
Hissing their song of the fortunate man
Who rests by wife and child at home
While November gusts. Needles, leaves,
And bits of trash, finding their motion
In sudden whirlwinds, wander the streets.
The plum and its vine, now stripped and wiry,
Huddle their warmth in the naked yard.
I gaze out the window as night comes on;
Sally reads; Schuyler asks to poke the fire.
Sparks like souls ascend the dark shaft.

Beyond our most immediate air,
Behind the ridge at evening's edge, the sun
Ignites the sky at its hem, and the sheerest
Garment we know goes up. Sleeves of flame
Extend toward the zenith; clouds like ingots
Heat and glow. Even the icy cirrus burn,
Fanned into coals, irradiating the upper air
As our windows flare and the whole sky twists.

To live within this involving flame,
We must be fire. Sally, we live by burning
Slowly, and know ourselves best
When we recognize the banked-up fires
In each other's eyes. I think of them
When the evening reddens, sky folding up
Like earth's last day. It gathers me
And lets me go, a nightly memento.

WAKING

Smearings of light, remembrance of music,
Interludes of hover and veer,
Then dim unlikely shapes appear—

Sheer white curtains lift at the window
As breezes clatter through twisting leaves
Flashing green and white. A landscape gathers,

Birds begin, and we in our bed
Both plunge again into total loss, loss
Of ourselves in our lives.

MARRIAGE FIRES

Where on the spectrum of living fire
Do a man and woman walk this morning
Through woods above a shallow river
Late in March? In winter they dozed
And smoldered coolly, or flared inside
Like ice on skin, a flame that numbs.
The grass lay matted and bleached by snow,
And so did they. She painted their walls
To peach or lavender, blocking the reach
Of clouds and plains, that white on white.
He traveled widely, books in his lap,
Sailing the floorlamp's pool of light.
They did not know they had been so sick,
But, convalescent, they slept together,
In each other's arms in separate dreams.

In the woods today the early blossoms
Shine like snow: bloodroot, snow drops,
Dutchman's breeches. The man and woman
Breathe cool air. They did not know
They had been asleep, but now
The sensation of slowly waking. The sky
Behind its lattice-work of empty branches
Starts to their eyes a different blue,
Like a run of music or sudden breeze
That lifts a curtain. Low bushes thrust out
Pointed leaves, green on one side,
Red on the other, little fires
Breaking out on the branch.

Which way shall they walk? The path
Divides. One trail rims a limestone bluff,
Climbing through cedars, then opens high
Where she wants to lead him, hand in hand.
She thinks of how the river looks,
Reflected sun from rippling shallows
Seeming to burn a thousand holes
In the world below. He wants to go down.
The other trail descends through hardwoods,
Skirting a creek. He remembers a pool
Where runoff floods have tumbled the rocks
And once he scooped up spheres of granite,
One in each hand, to strike together
And hear them ring. Though water flew,
He saw their spark, saw the arc that tracked
A glowing chip and smelled like smoke.
So they stand at the branch, each holding
In mind a different way. They do not know
Both end in fire.

TWO OR THREE DREAMS OF SPRING

I.

I step out onto
The open porch,
The long waiting

Finally over.
An all night rain
Has melted the snow,

The glassy mounds,
And water stands
In stunned, brown grass.

The first mild
Breezes smell like earth.
The flowering crab

(Was it always there
In the center of the yard?)
Is already open!

I lean against
The wooden porch-rail,
Take a deep breath,

Then wake in the dark—
Rub a hole with my fist
On frosted glass,

Look out on drifts.

2.

I am out on the porch;
The long waiting
Is finally over.

Loose water pools
In greening grass.
The air smells of earth.

Warm breezes tangle
Purple lilacs,
Whitening crabs.

Can this be a dream?
I rap my knuckles
Hard on the rail.

It hurts; it is real.
Then I wake, look out—
Hunched shoulders

Of snow.

3.

On the far side of town
A thin, green fog—
The first split buds.

Nearer, a maple,
Its catkins hanging
Like Spanish earrings.

And the grass, having sipped
Its snowdrifts down,
Burns green as Ireland

While tulips burn
In their bed by the porch
An unearthly red,

A red that wounds
As a way to heal.
Can this be real?

Can this be real?

BLACK VELVET

Cars lunge into the city,
Four abreast and pushing seventy.

Night's seductions draw us in.
Red streaks glow where the sun has fallen

On blackened stacks. Glittering turrets
Blaze at evening, towers of commerce

Burly-shouldered and empty-eyed.
Lit apartments hang their gardens against the sky.

Traffic hums in its usual groove.
I glide with the others, homing through

Toward familiar rooms. Halfway there
The billboard rises. Its brilliant square

Presents a woman in evening dress
Reclining by two glasses, ice,

And the opened bottle. She fingers
Its neck. The gesture lingers

As her level gaze
Attracts my eyes.

Here, in public, in a private car,
Fill the scene with your own desire:

Ceremonial drinks, two voices rubbing
Like bow and string,

The alcohol whispering,
Senses, velvet, extending dark wings.

I wince at the wrong,
The same old come-on,

Women arranged by men and dollars
In poses drawn from early masters,

But sweeping around this curve in the dark—
Her form suspended, a park

Erected among the buildings
That light the city, stacked and burning—

I always look, each nightly trip,
From shoulder to waist

To the dangerous swerve of the hip.

SIGHT AND DISTANCE

Afternoon like a crystal box: pine trees,
       citizens, rising clouds
       in shining cases.

Finches dart through walnut branches,
       through scissoring light,
Specimens perfect, air like glass.

But I'm all eyes and no hands—
Things flash and recede.

The sun goes down and evening buffs
       its copper brighter.

Lights snap on at the tops of poles
And insects madden, circling globes.

Bats and swallows veer and feed,
       veer and feed,
As night hawks dive, their gullets open.

Dark descends to gorge itself on the gorgeous Earth.

Darling, touch me. I'm almost here.

LIBRETTO FOR THE FALL OF THE YEAR

Except for the red oak's splash,
an occasional jay,
or the breeze
                sliced
by the sumac leaves,
the trees have been empty for days.

Our vision's cleared.
                        Now we see
all the way to the lake.
                        Light rips
the water at the wave tips,
cuts bright doors in the town's west edge.

That's where we want to go, Sally,
out to the lake
to cruise on the jingling sparks,
canoe like the fools
we are for the lightning
                        rippling
slowly like fat water snakes on the swells.

*

Dip oar

and the water whorls at its blade
like a shoulder flexing.
                        We
and the lake pull by.

                        Reflections
quiver, slip with our strokes. The roads
and the trees, we ourselves
fan out in
waves from the prow. Your hair
and a road wind trellised in the limbs.
Where does the body end?

*

This is the road I'll take, gone
blond with dust.
                    I'll stroke,
You steer.
                We'll ride on out
that lithe geometry of water lights.

Remember this: we've named the fall
a clearing. Pull
for the bright west edge.

WINTER IN EDEN

There are no fences, no gates in the snowy
Fields and wrecked orchards; only the sword-blade

Winter light swings north to south, east to west
Where the straight horizon locks itself with ice

To a sky too bright to look at. We are free
Among the trees of knowledge, gleaning

Shriveled apples and berries, sweet
As they melt in our hot mouths. Memory

Flares as we walk beneath the torn limbs.
At home each night the dream arrives, insistent

As a chanted word: the slim trunk rises,
Branches dense with scalloped leaves protecting

Their fruit—globes the colors of perfect bodies,
Naked, shameless in the tree of life.

INTO THE NEW WORLD

—for David Wyatt

Near dawn, in Harlem, steam rises from manhole covers, and
    a woman sweeps one square of sidewalk, a chosen place
        again and again.

It has been five weeks. At Canal the police
    have closed off traffic and the streets stand empty
        all the way to Murray.
        A glimpse through the gate:

            that unblocked sun,
            that scorched black cube
            maybe ten stories high,
            jagged spars of façade thrusting up.

    The ground by the fence has been swept clean.
            The wind, that dust—

I walk east, then south. The fence at Fulton has been blown down—
    a cop explains, "All these flags act like sails."

Maiden Lane and Broadway: a small crowd watches backhoes work.
        Sun glints off the
        compressed metal cube—
        flayed steel.
    A worker says, "Go one block south, then over to West."
        Farther down the odor is stronger.

Then another glimpse:
        blackened girders like Gothic arches,

      like bombed Cologne.
      Jets of water cool the ruins.

On the Hudson, whitecaps. I walk along the soothing river.

At West and Warren where dump trucks leave the dusty site,
   men hose them down.
         All work will stop for a finger bone,
         for an improvised rite.

           What wind is this, what dust?

  Warren takes me back to Greenwich and I've gone around.

*

In Mecca's heart the Kaaba stands,
        another black box
   where pilgrims circle—
      the long journey, then seven times
      around that center, itself impenetrable.

    The holy is not locatable.
          Still,
  one longs for a spot.

DISASTER MOVIES

There's something in me that loves disaster.
I pay to see my worst fears, titanic
In the dark, play out on a screen larger
Than life, then hit the streets, renewed, intact—

Especially in the '70s, when Shelley Winters
And Ernest Borgnine, sweaty & plump, navigated
The tipped ship where Hackman swung from stairs
And fell. Liddy had burgled the Watergate

But I left *Poseidon* serene as Nixon
Alone with Brezhnev or sitting with Mao.
Dean took him down and Ford did the pardon.
A disaster movie? I want to go. I love how

I burn in my seat, a towering inferno,
Then stroll through the dark, aglow.

JAN BRUEGHEL THE ELDER'S
A WOODLAND ROAD WITH TRAVELERS

Midway in their desperate journey they
Find themselves in a dark wood. Women
In skirts and domed hats carry heavy
Jugs and stuffed baskets, all they now own.

Men drive beasts, pigs on leashes, horses tethered
To a wagon tipping, too full of nothing
Terribly valuable. At least today the weather
Clears at last. One woman quietly sings.

About suffering we are always wrong
These days. In Brueghel's painting we peer
From the woods; the travelers' backs, strong
But bent, are what we see as they steer

Themselves toward a distant city. I am in that city
And watch them coming. Their faces don't scare me.

NOT WITH A BANG, BUT A TWEET

Fourteen, one-forty—what's the difference
Besides concision? Lines, characters, syllables,
It's all just counting (0101). Sense
Spills through little tubes its billion baubles.

Until it doesn't. We, the fat, fail. The grid
Fails, satellites fall. We thumb dumb texts
To a sky that does not answer. Even God
Looks away. Our guns don't save us. What's next?

Outside, first, the traffic, actual, smelly.
And grass—the beautiful uncut hair of graves.
So nature again, and death, and people yelling,
Vibrating air. Then the sky sizzles and it all caves

To the artist incising with sharpened bone
Her bison—those next one hundred forty strokes.

ON FORSYTHIA OVERHANGING A SLATE WALL

Forsythia sprawls from a central bang.
Branches arc light delight, as if to map
Trajectories of the heart. When the sap
Knocks in its pipes, the yellow blossoms swing
Like suns, brief trumpets loud with their light
Squeezed out from a branch of the void. Suns cool
Then drop like blossoms or cities into the pool
That can't be ruffled and reflects no light.

This bush shows how, by resistance, lives are built.
Forsythia—slow fountain—drills for the heart,
Taps capillary rills and pumps rich silt,
Finds rhymes in the leaves' green labs, knots dirt
And sunlight tight, and over this slate wall
Slows water to a lobed and tendrilled fall.

II

GETTYSBURG

The real war will never get in the books.
                    —Walt Whitman

But the real books will always be filled with leaves,
And real leaves have always grown from the dead,
So the dead will always return in the books.

The dead, beloved, continue to speak in the leaves,
And the leaves of the book continue to green with the dead,
And the bronze leaves of the great book lie still
        beneath the copse of trees.

AMULET

A polished copper plate. Silver, mercury, iodine crystals. Light
Traveled from her and was fixed. The little mirror remembers.

He sits on the grass, in sun. Like so many leaves
The men have fallen. His eyes are mirrors that remember—

Miller's cornfield, Dunker Church, the Sunken Road
Called Bloody Lane. Mirrors, exposed, remember.

A ball is in his thigh, and the ground where he sits
Receives his blood like a mirror that will remember.

From around his neck he removes his Beloved. The clasp
Ticks, the amulet opens, and the mirror inside remembers

The day, three autumns before, when light from her face,
Resplendent, stayed. Here, in his hand, the mirror remembers.

In a certain light he can see himself in the metal disc,
His face beneath hers. The mirror holds him, remembers.

NECKLACE WITH DAGUERREOTYPE

Yesterday fog. Today, near Lookout Mountain, lost both
My hospital and all its wounded. The North is in the South

And I must go where needed. I grow used to death;
Its rags and bones are no longer men. We march north, south—

But always farther from you. Our terrible path
Tunnels deeper in hell. North or South,

It is all one place. We fill the cornfields with death
And worse. I have had enough of North and South.

A little world cunningly made is a clod of earth
When the grape shot hits. They fall the same, South and North.

*

We retire for a while to Atlanta. I have lost my faith
In this war, think always of you, my whole and only South.

Had my picture made—a life mirror—and send it with
My love. (Pike, who was wounded, carries it south.)

Open the locket and find me. The shining disc is my oath.
Do you see yourself in its depth—you south, me north?

Now that I can sleep again I dream of your mouth.
I dream you to bed, kiss you north and south.

*

First light. I lie in my cot and spy above me a speckled moth.
Did it flutter through my tent flaps from north or south?

IN VIETNAM

The ground remembers.
The rice paddy
Holds its shoots,
Yields full bowls
From the bomb
Crater rice paddy,
The ground remembers.

DRIFTING SOULS

This narrow photo one hand-span
Wide contains a landscape
Pock-marked, cracked, stained tan

Like smoke. Within it figures wrapped
In dust stand fixed in sight
As if inside a rifle's scope.

But for now they will not die
And are not killing, only shuffling
Through grasses, light as ghosts—mild,

Becalmed. Fifty years is as nothing
Here, where they linger, fastened,
Their legs disappearing

In uncut grass, their torsos thickened
By packs, canteens, by radios, guns,
Pursuing their endless errand.

CAMOUFLAGE

I fight the war. Choppers painted in camouflage
Drop me at the map's coordinates. I land
In jungle, in the deep shit. In Vietnam
Everything's different—"the American war"
They say over here, and strange beauty hides
The danger where Charlie lurks. I wear leaves

On my helmet, put my faith in leaves
To keep me safe. I trim myself in camouflage
And dress in swirling shades of green to hide
In fractured light. I disappear in the land
And can't be found, a casualty of war
Before I'm gone, a ghost that stalks Vietnam.

Though I may have vanished, in South Vietnam
I drift among trees, the grasses, leaves.
From village to village I carry war
With my radio and my camouflage,
An agent of the inscrutable West, land
Of the blunt instrument. No-one hides

From a B-52, and no-one hides
When I call down jets to burn Vietnam
To save it. I call down fire and the land
Receives my stroke. My boot-heel falls, leaves
Bomb craters. Only decades will camouflage
The wide gouges—rice paddies after the war.

What is the moral equivalent of war?
I can't remember. The rain comes and hides

The details. Here and now, in my camouflage,
I am the god of hell-fire, and Vietnam
Holds me tight. Its jungle of reasons leaves
Me blank. I follow orders. Where choppers land

I pitch my camp. Sometimes it seems the land
Itself is the foreign thing we fight. We war
Against trees, hit strange, offending leaves
With Agent Orange and kerosene. When hides
Appear—canopied trails that wind Vietnam—
Night descends to spread its darker camouflage.

We fight the land where the enemy hides.
Somewhere there isn't war, but in Vietnam
It's dawn. The leaves put on their camouflage.

GREEN MAN

In the jungle war
He became its leaves,
Camouflaged by what he wore.
In the jungle war
He fell in his second tour.
His wife still grieves.
In the jungle war
He became its leaves.

VIETNAM VETERANS MEMORIAL, NIGHT

To the left the spotlit Washington Monument
Jabs the air, progenitive, white;
Beyond trees, to the right, the stonework glows
Where Lincoln broods in his marble seat;

And here, between, in the humid dark,
Where curving pathways lead and branch,
Sally and I step forward carefully
Somewhere near the open trench.

Choppers shuttle across the sky
With jets for National crying down,
But we've lost our way. The intricate dark
In the center of town moves all around.

There are others here: white T-shirts drift
In heavy air. Then three bronze soldiers
Caught in floodlights across the field
Stare hard at where we want to go.

From above we find the wall's far end
And begin to descend. Ahead of us
Soft footlights brush the lustered stone,
Dim figures trace their hands across

The rows of letters, and others, hushed,
File past in the dark. At first we are only
Ankle deep in the names of the dead,
But the path slopes down. Quietly,

We wade on in. In the depths beside
The lit inscription, men and women
Hold each other, mortal, drowning.
Many have stopped at a chosen station

To touch an absence carved away.
From deep inside the chiseled panels
Particular deaths rush out at them.
The minds of veterans gape like tunnels

To burning huts. We are over our heads.
Now Sally turns, sobs hard, and stops.
We cling to each other like all the rest
And climb away with altered steps.

KHMER ROUGE

If you wore glasses, if you drank milk—
Showed signs of learning or foreign habits—
You were impure. They said of thousands,
"Spare them, no profit; remove them, no loss."

Show signs of learning or foreign habits
And they sent you out to dig canals.
"Spare them, no profit; remove them, no loss"—
The motto emptied cities. In "year zero"

They sent thousands out to dig canals,
Directing floods for the great harvest.
In year zero a motto emptied cities,
Filled Tuol Sleng and the killing fields.

They directed floods in a great harvest;
They said to thousands, "You are impure."
You were sent to prison or the killing fields
If you wore glasses, if you drank milk.

THE PHOTOGRAPHED

The soon-to-be-dead
were photographed, filed—
two boys, a girl, with tags
on their shirts, numbers

of the photographed filed
in metal drawers,
numbered by the tags on shirts
to be kept in order,

kept in drawers
by men who killed
for a kind of order,
for purity and clear ideas.

The men who killed—
two million gone
for purity and clear ideas—
trenched mass graves

where two million
sank into earth,
into shallow trenches, graves
of mingled bones.

They sank into earth
and the dirt took them,
mingled their bones
and sent them back.

The dirt took them
into its dark
and sent them back
in caladium leaves

that rose from dark
and reached for sunlight,
caladium leaves
whose bitten faces

reached for sunlight,
and here they are—
the bitten faces
fleshed in green.

And here they are,
two boys, a girl, with tags,
newly fleshed in green,
the soon to be dead.

DUTY

Nhem En, working as a photographer under the direction of superintendent Kaing Guek Eav (Duch), took portraits of men, women, and children processed into the S21/Tuol Sleng prison, where virtually all of the approximately 14,000 inmates were interrogated, tortured, and killed.

"I was 9 when they gave me a drum. We sang and marched,
A children's band that toured the villages before I took pictures.

'Oh, Angka, we deeply love you, we resolve to follow your red way . . .'
I beat my drum and the cadre smiled when he took our picture.

Duch liked me. I'm clean and I filed the photos well.
He gave me a Rolex watch. If I'd lost a picture

I would have been killed. (Later, when I ran, I traded the watch
For rice.) I was following orders when I took the pictures.

I was 16. She had full lips, black hair, dark eyes. I pinned the number
To the front of her shirt, number 21. It was my duty to take the picture.

One had a name—she was someone's wife—with a tiny baby
In the crook of her arm. What was my duty? I took the picture."

I peer through the gaze of his lens. They seem to stare at me now,
But then they saw him, a teenage boy who took their pictures.

Later the screams from inner rooms. For three years—
Communal breakfast, then new arrivals, the taking of pictures.

"They arrived in blindfolds. I had to remove the cloth. 'Where am I?'
They asked, and 'What have I done?' Preparing to take the picture,

I only told them, 'Look straight ahead. Don't lean your head
To the left or right.' I had to say this so the picture

Would turn out right." He pointed the camera, adjusted the lights.
"The duty of the photographer is just to take the picture."

UP FROM ITS GROUND THE WATER

Up from its ground the water
Climbs beneath dry bark

Out from stiff buds the new leaves press
When the Earth tilts

From crowded graves the dead surge
We see them now

In the flesh of leaves
Their faces rise

THE BOTANY OF TUOL SLENG

They stir and rise. Again
The captives find their way
To confront the light.
Shoot them quickly, before

The captives find their way
To say what we do.
Shoot them quickly, before
They stir and rise again.

THE CHANKIRI TREE

At the killing field, Choeng Ek, no bells are rung.
In a tall stupa, piled skulls cannot blame or resent
This staring crowd—emptied bones without tongues.

Pathways lead between excavations begun
And abandoned. The plain is scarred with shallow dents
Bordered by trees where children climb the rungs.

In a low building, victims' photos, hung
In rows of black and white, draw the murdered present.
I scan across the peering eyes, struck dumb.

Back outside in the glaring sun, leaves are stung
With images—faces risen, called up and sent
To green the tree of knowledge rung by rung.

See, they return: In the wide ditch new grass has sprung
Where bones still lie, shaded by the tree's broad tent.
When a breeze moves, leaves whisper what they've become.

The bark is torn. Against this trunk executioners flung
The bodies of children. Bullets, costly, were rarely spent.
We climb the tree of knowledge rung by rung.
O I perceive after all so many uttering tongues.

FLOWERS OF THE FIELD

Children peer from nasturtium leaves,
cheek, nose, eye, or temple marked
by the spot where the stem attached.
"A single blow fissured glass
and marked my face with its one
blemish. This nasturtium leaf, new
in spring, is the pane through which
I peer at you."
                        What shall I cry?
All flesh is grass; it passes away
with the flowers of the field.
The word alone or an image abides,
our meeting place, this one
new leaf arisen.

III

THE VARIETIES OF RELIGIOUS EXPERIENCE

—Out of William James

1.

God is great; we know not His ways.
What we think we own He takes from us.

Possess your soul in patience.
We may pass the valley of the shadow
or we may not!

After deliverance,
sparrowlike,
we twitter and hop, quickly forgetting
the imminent hawk on the bough.

Lie low, lie low,
for you rest in the hands of a living God.

2.

Experience consists of a conscious field,
plus a thing known, plus an attitude towards it,
plus a sense of the self that knows.

This is the bit, small though it be, that is solid
as long as it lasts. And on these bits—
on such push and pinch—a life is made,
and destiny rolls on fortune's wheels
on a line connecting real events.

Yet all the while, beyond farther limits,
beyond the sensible, beyond understanding,
our beings plunge.
We close our mouths
and are as nothing
in the floods and waterspouts of God.

THE HIGHEST EMBLEM IN THIS CIPHER OF THE WORLD

—Out of Emerson

The circle is the highest emblem
in this cipher of a world.
                        Standing in a field,
the eye scans the horizon, the clock's hand sweeps,
and the effort of thought presses out a wave,
forms a ridge on which we heap our rules,
our rites and usage. So we build a wall
to hem in life.
              But the quick soul
bursts through.
              There is no outside, no enclosing wall,
no circumference to us,
                        only wheel beyond wheel.

In common hours we sit statuesque. We wait,
empty, the mighty symbols that surround us always
seeming prose and toys.
                    Then the god comes.
By a flash of his eye he burns away
the shrouding veils. We statues live
and the meanings of even the furniture clear—
of the cup and saucer, of the table,
the clock and its dial.

                    People wish to be settled,
but the ground on which we stand
slides. All that was solid shakes and rattles;

foundations dance. Only unsettled
do we live in hope.
                        Our way of life is wonder-filled:
Abandonment, it whispers to us.
                              No love can be bound
by secure oath against higher love. The heart refuses
to be imprisoned.

       No man, no woman—
if truth is in him, if the god has touched her—
will be fully known. The last chamber,
the final closet will remain unopened.

We scale a mysterious ladder.
Rung by rung, it points the way
to the unattainable flying Perfect.

In this cipher of a world, the circle is
the highest emblem.
                The field cannot be seen
from the field. A striding center,
I step on horizons.

THOREAU, IN SPRING, AT THE RAILWAY EMBANKMENT

—*Out of* Walden

In a spring thaw, sand flows down
the railway embankment, lava
over snow; streams overlap,
strands interlace, obeying
halfway the laws of currents,
halfway the laws of foliage.
I see vegetable forms in iron
colors—brown, gray, reddish,
yellowish—vines tangling,
acanthus, chicory. I see sprays
of leaves, sap-filled, pulpy,
fans spreading like reef coral,
like nets of nerves. Thick
stalactites gleam in sunlight,
their cave exposed. I think
I stand in the Artist's lab
who made the world and is still
at work, sporting on this bank,
strewing designs. This is frost
coming out of the ground, this
is the Spring.
                The Maker
of this earth but patented a leaf:
the whole tree is a single
leaf, its branches veins,
and rivers are still vaster
leaves whose pulp is earth.

Even ice grows crystal leaves,
as if water learned from water plants.
No wonder the earth
expresses itself in leaves,
it labors so with the thought
of them.
          The earth is not
dead history, stratum on stratum.
It is living poetry, green leaves
preceding flowers, preceding
fruit—the soul's delight.
Sand flows from a railway
embankment: this is the frost
coming out in March,
this is the world becoming.

CHANTICLEER

Chanticleer in the unchinked cabin
Cries this morning: *I desire to speak*
In a waking moment to men awake.

Sit in my doorway and watch with me:
The fire-ball sun climbs the pine tree rungs.
Night mists lift from the pond like veils.

Throw off the sleep that veils your eyes.
We could entertain a goddess here,
Auroral all day with a dawning in us.

He ends his call—*Wake up! Wake up!*—
As the sun cuts through.
                              I hide my face.
The light that puts out sight is darkness.

THE BUTTERFLY PORTRAIT

In the portrait, his favorite, Whitman
in slouch hat, cardigan, beard,
regards a butterfly perched on his finger,

Spring, '77, in Curtis Taylor's lens.
Yes, it was real, he told a friend. *I've always
had a knack of attracting critters.*

It was not. The cardboard prop
was fastened in place with wire.
Later the poet, chair-bound in Camden,

let his papers fall like leaves around him.
(As Archie said, autumn trees
"stand in pools of themselves.")

Whitman in his rocker left piles unstacked
in natural disorder and told a visitor,
What I need comes to hand.

But he kept his paper butterfly near,
packed in a box—chrysalis or coffin—
for others to find:

*I laid in my stores in advance;
I considered long and seriously of you
before you were born.*

Photographer's prop and poet's trope,
it's a little book—two leaves,
four pages—painted on the bottom

and printed on top with an Easter verse;
    THE FIRST BEGOTTEN OF THE DEAD
    FOR US HE ROSE, OUR GLORIOUS HEAD . . . .

"The poet nothing affirmeth, and therefore
never lieth." But he lied and affirmed:
the critter was paper, and paper

lives—*who touches this, touches a man.*
And the Eastern Tiger Swallowtail
that nectars a lily, yellow and black

in my garden this morning, emerged
and clung to its cracked tomb
just days ago, pumping its wings,

readying for flight, its colors stiffening.

IV

THE MORNING NEWS

This is how the future arrives:
The web announces three hundred dead,
A great heart holds their cancelled lives

In brilliant air, the public grieves,
Then the next blow comes. Our nerves go bad,
But this is how the future arrives.

Morning by morning the planet dives
From dark to light still sheathed in blood.
Some great heart may hold their lives,

But we did not know them, husbands and wives
Who plunged last night to a final bed.
This is how the future arrives

And we fight it off. We cannot give
Ourselves to them, can only plead
That some great heart hold all their lives.

A nearing moment balanced on knives
Points hard at us. Dawn wears red.
This is how the future arrives.
May some great heart hold all our lives.

ELEGY

Everything dies, baby, that's a fact,
But maybe everything that dies someday comes back.
Put your make-up on, fix your hair up pretty,
And meet me tonight in Atlantic City.
—Bruce Springsteen

On this bench by a fountain, pattern matters.
Water arcs from green brass like a tree
Branches, hangs for a moment, then falls and shatters

In the fountain pan, dispersing like leaves
In soil; then it's drawn back up through dark
Pipes to be thrown again into sunlight. Trees

Around it trace slower patterns. Beneath their bark,
Springs rise. Oaks are fountains, their leaves
Pressing out, and willows are fountains. The park's

Gardens bloom and fail, rising with apparent ease
And falling with grace. Flowers throw brief coronets;
Geranium blossoms fall like memories

Left with friends, the ones who will not forget.
Like leaves our flesh grows old and withers;
Like water it rose—bright jets.

THE DAY AFTER CHARLOTTESVILLE
WE DECIDE TO DIG OUT THE QUINCE

The day after Charlottesville, Twenty-Seventeen, we decide finally
    to dig out the quince.
We chose it ourselves for a showy corner of the lot, but it spread,
    thorny, painful to prune, its tiny flowers and hard fruit
    not what we had imagined.
First to go is the green top, lopped and tossed, easily cut, revealing
    knots of thumb-thick trunks—dozens of them—and pencil-sized
    runners, spreading, reaching.
We knew this would be hard, had been putting it off, waiting for
    a cool morning, less Virginia sun. Now we grub
With spade and shovel, then jab sharp hoes to pick packed dirt from
    between gnarled roots that plunge, tangle, grip rocks
    and clods and their brethren.
Soon we are breathless, sweat stings our eyes. Relentless
    shrub—primitive apple—even its lowest distant twigs sprout
    swelling buds, pink clenching yellow stamens.
"Slow down," Sally tells me. I keep chopping, gasping. I wanted
    this, something hard and local.
On the phone David said, "Civil wars never end."
Angry, weeping, I see torchlit faces, hear "blood and soil," see
    Deandre Harris beaten with poles and Heather Heyer
    murdered in the street.
Sally touches my shoulder. I sob and straighten. An ache
    in my throat answers hate with hate—
Mother Emanuel, forgive me.

Next day we trench around knotted roots and hit them
    with the hose. Dirt blasts away, showing
    deeper runners in hard red clay.

When the ground has dried I fire the bristling stump
        with a torch, then batter charred sticks with an axe.
Embers cool, then it's time, again, to dig. Far down, I hope,
        these roots narrow to a single tap we can reach and sever
        or pull entire.

Friends, we could not reach the bottom. It went down and down.

IN A FIELD OF WEEDS

Man is but a reed, the weakest in nature, but he is
a thinking reed.
     —Pascal

Five degrees. Rough, shifting winds. Sunlight crashing
Almost audibly, sky to snow-pack, snow-pack to sky.
Eyes shrink hard to their smallest stop, but winter drills in.
Brilliant splinters of ice in the air blow up and down.

In the polished field stiff weeds poke through like rusty wire.
Stems and branches, anchored in ice, shake hard with gusts,
Knock stalk on stalk and litter the snow with broken reeds.
Detritus lifts in a whirl of air, then lies back down.

Hollow weeds rattle bone on bone, and the man who listens
Slowly turns to scan the rim of an icy zero. Acres of snow
Reach every way. Sunlight fills the blinding page.
He has come out here to read what it says, and he thinks he knows.

He walks back home and remembers everything;
Everything holds in his icy mirror. When words arrive
He chooses those which fabricate nothing, take nothing away.
I read the words on the snowy page and they stick like burrs.

They name the terror and make it flower. We stand together.

ANALYSIS

Hefting the axe-head,
Throwing it down through
Oak's red heart,

I wonder and swing,
The wide blue day opening
Worlds within worlds

In winter branches,
In shadowy centers
Of boxwood shrubs

Where the quick eye lingers,
Curious after the hidden
Root of what it sees

And hardly believes:
A globe of living forms
Afloat in glittering air.

The steel head cleaves
Fragrant slabs from rounds,
Uncasking intoxicants—

Wood's bouquet like
Burgundy aged
In the innermost rings.

Slabs clatter;
Kindling splits

With a few more strokes;

But still red oak holds
Tight in its grain
A bottomless space

Where planets swish
And imagination dives in vain
For grounding or platform.

Meanwhile, back in the bluish
Light of early December,
Two imparadised birds

Are whistling, hidden in pines,
And deep inside a whorl
Of hardwood, blade against burl,

The axe-head rests.
I pry and hammer, pry
'Til the splitting handle snaps,

Then carry the whole
With its swallowed wedge
Back home to my grate,

Where the knot I could not
Break with my axe,
The fire unties.

NOTE

"When the Magnitude of the Possible Dawned," part 3, draws from two newspaper articles and a book about the Hiroshima and Nagasaki bombings: "A Final Accounting of the Death and Destruction," by Kai Erikson, a review in the August 9, 1981 *New York Times Book Review* of *Hiroshima and Nagasaki: The Physical, Medical, and Social Effects of the Atomic Bombings,* by The Committee for the Compilation of Materials on Damage Caused by the Atomic Bombs in Hiroshima and Nagasaki, translated by Eisei Ishikawa and David L. Swain (New York: Basic Books, 1981); "The Bomb and the Remembering," by Liz Nakaara in the August 6, 1981 *Washington Post;* and *Unforgettable Fire: Pictures Drawn by Atomic Bomb Survivors,* ed. by Japan Broadcasting Corporation (New York: Pantheon, 1981).

ACKNOWLEDGMENTS

The author gratefully acknowledges previous publishers of work included in this book:

Able Muse: "The Butterfly Portrait."

Diode: "Up from its Ground the Water" (as "Ancestral Altar, no. 16"), "Duty," "Flowers of the Field."

The Hollins Critic: "The Varieties of Religious Experience."

The Hudson Review: "The Highest Emblem in this Cipher of a World," "Winter in Eden," "Black Velvet," "Vietnam Veterans Memorial, Night," "When the Magnitude of the Possible Dawned."

The New York Quarterly: "Into the New World."

The Northwest Review: "Camouflage."

Prime Number: "The Day After Charlottesville We Dig out the Quince."

Scribner's Best American Poetry blog: "Drifting Souls," "Not with a Bang but a Tweet."

Subtropics: "The Botany of Tuol Sleng," "In Vietnam."

Thrush: "Elegy."

Virginia Quarterly Review: "Khmer Rouge," "Ancestral Altar, no. 7" (now titled "The Photographed"), "The Chankiri Tree," "The Morning News."

Washington Square: "Thoreau, in Spring, at the Railway Embankment."

"The Chankiri Tree" appeared in the anthology *Villanelles* (New York, NY: Knopf, 2012) and in *Binh Danh*, an exhibition catalog published by the Eleanor D. Wilson Museum of Art at Hollins University (February

ACKNOWLEDGMENTS

2009). "Vietnam Veterans Memorial, Night," has been reprinted in *Retellings: A Thematic Literature Anthology* (New York, NY: McGraw-Hill, 2004) and in *Carrying the Branch: Poets in Search of Peace* (Glenview, IL: Glass Lyre Press, LLC, 2017).

"Libretto for the Fall of the Year" was included in the fine art chapbook *Vein Along the Fault* (Brooktondale, NY: The Laueroc Press, 1979).

Several poems are drawn from the chapbook *Ancestral Altars* (Charlottesville, VA: Artist's Proof Editions, 2015): "Khmer Rouge," "The Photographed" (as "Ancestral Altar, no. 7"), "Up from its Ground the Water" (as "Ancestral Altar, no. 16"), "The Chankiri Tree," "The Botany of Tuol Sleng," "In Vietnam," "Drifting Souls," "Duty," "Flowers of the Field," and "This Daguerreotype of Skulls."

The following poems were included in the limited-edition book, *Winter in Eden* (Farragut, IA: Loess Hills Books, 1997): "The Morning News," "Chanticleer," "In a Field of Weeds," "Winter in Eden," "Black Velvet," "When the Magnitude of the Possible Dawned," and "Vietnam Veterans Memorial, Night."

This book was set in Mrs. Eaves, designed by Slovak typographer Zuzana Licko in 1996. The founder of the renowned firm, Émigré Graphics, Licko decided with this font to take on the challenge of re-interpreting the classic Baskerville typeface, originally created in the 1750s. Mrs. Eaves has been described as sometimes "awkward" but also possessing "an undefined quality that resonates with people." It is named after Sarah Eaves, originally William Baskerville's housekeeper, whom he later married.

This book was designed by Shannon Carter, Ian Creeger, and Gregory Wolfe. It was published in hardcover, paperback, and electronic formats by Slant Books, Seattle, Washington.

www.ingramcontent.com/pod-product-compliance
Lightning Source LLC
Chambersburg PA
CBHW051700040426
42446CB00009B/1236